Meeting Attractive Women

A Nice Guys and Players Book

Meeting Attractive Women

A Nice Guys and Players Book

Rom Wills
Wills Publishing

Meeting Attractive Women
A Nice Guys and Players Book

Copyright 2005, 2014
by
Romuald P. Wills

ALL RIGHTS RESERVED
No part of this book may be reproduced, stored in a retrieval system, or transmitted in any form or by any means electronic or mechanical or whatsoever, including voice recordings, without the express, prior, written permission from:

Romuald P. Wills
romwills@aol.com

ISBN-13 978-0692223284
ISBN-10 0692223282

To my sons.

Also by Rom Wills

Nice Guys and Players
Sexual Chemistry
Starting From Zero

Table of Contents

Introduction 9

Profile of the Attractive Woman 12

Development Plan for Men 16

Meeting Attractive Women Made Simple 43

Going for the Best...............................…....58

Appendix I – A Woman's Choice................61

Appendix II – Secrets of the Select…............69

Introduction

You are walking down the street minding your business when all of a sudden a thunderbolt hits you. Walking towards you is a woman so beautiful, so sexy your breath becomes shallow. Your mind starts running through different methods to meet this woman. The woman gets closer to you, smiles slightly and walks past you. You turn and look at her walking away thinking she has a nice booty. That evening you do one of three things: sit at home by yourself wondering how come you didn't say anything; hang out with a group of friends who are telling you what they would have done in that situation; go to an Internet message board where other equally frustrated men tell you what you should have done. Having experienced this and other scenarios is probably why you are reading this book.

Let's face reality. Men are not buying dating and seduction books to win the love of the homely girl who might make the best wife. Men are not frequenting message boards and shelling out thousands of dollars to learn the inner workings of a woman 100 pounds overweight with a pleasant personality. Men want to learn how to get with the attractive woman, the dyme, the HB10, the hot babe; you know what I'm talking about. In this book I will tell you how to meet and deal with the Attractive Woman in a way that's in line with the principles I presented in **Nice Guys and Players** and **Sexual Chemistry**. My books focused on self-improvement in a real world manner. I didn't provide lines or special methods because tricks are for kids and I write for MEN. As I will explain later the best way to get an Attractive Woman is to be an Attractive Man.

One thing my books didn't focus on to a great extent was how to meet a woman. The reason is that too often a man will want beautiful women but after being constantly rejected, complain about these women like the women are the ones with the problem. He will not stop to consider that the ONLY thing these women had in common was him. A man needs to develop himself before trying to get any woman.

This book, though small, will provide three basic things: a general profile of Attractive Women based on my personal observations; the traits a man must have to appeal specifically to these women; ways to effectively approach and meet these beautiful women.

One final note before I begin. As noted this is a small book. One issue I have with the whole dating book market is that everything is made to seem complicated. It's not! As you will see, meeting Attractive Women is actually very easy. It's the men themselves who make the process hard. It's not rocket science. It's one of the most primal things on the planet. It's our own fears that mess everything up.

Profile of the Attractive Woman

One thing to consider in describing the Attractive Woman is the old adage, "beauty is in the eye of the beholder." In other words what is beautiful and attractive to one man is butt ugly to another man. For example, to a white man from a solid middle class background, the epitome of beauty is a slim woman with a pretty face and big breasts. A Black man from a poor background may consider a woman with a big round butt to be extremely attractive even though her face and breasts are plain.

I define an Attractive Woman as first someone whose appeal crosses racial, nationality, and socio-economic boundaries. She can walk into a room with men of all races and backgrounds and most of them would find her attractive. The woman will most likely have an hourglass figure, which is the most universally desirable female shape. Her body will tend to be mesomorphic – not skinny but not fat. Her facial features will be decidedly feminine. Her physical features are the first consideration as men are visual creatures and no amount of political correctness or social engineering is going to change this reality.

The second trait to consider is their persona. The most common thing I've found with Attractive Women is that they have distinctly feminine personas. In fact, I would argue that it's their persona that makes them attractive. We've all seen women who had the physical features of an Attractive Woman. They had the pretty face and body, but we still didn't feel that jolt. In some cases we managed to meet and date them anyway but something was still missing. We found that the women were cold and mean. Let me share a piece of wisdom: the thing that makes someone attractive, female or male, is not the physical package though this is very important. What makes someone attractive is his or her inner qualities. For example, you have identical twin girls with beautiful faces and shapely bodies. Yet one is considered a seven while the other is considered a ten. Why is this when they are physically identical? The seven keeps a mean look on her face. She wears her hair in a bun and wears loose clothing which hides her figure. The seven also behaves in a slightly masculine manner. The ten on the other hand wears her hair out and has light makeup and lipstick. The ten wears clothing and shoes that show off her body shape. Finally, the ten behaves in a decidedly feminine manner.

So we have thus defined an Attractive Woman as someone with a universally pleasing bone and body structure enhanced by a distinctly feminine persona. The third piece of the puzzle relates to her personal interests. The stereotypes of Attractive Women are that they are airheads with nothing better to do but sit around and look good. I have yet to meet an Attractive Woman with nothing going on upstairs. It may seem that way initially. You happen to get into a conversation with a beautiful woman and quite frankly she has nothing to say. You immediately think she's an airhead. What really happened is that society projects certain personality traits onto Attractive Women and attractive men as well. Society says that these beautiful people are vain and shallow. So when one meets an Attractive Woman the expectation is that she is shallow. Thus your conversation will only touch on shallow subjects because that's your expectation. The conversation will probably stay shallow until the woman decides to discuss deeper subjects.

The point is that Attractive Women have the same interests as other people. I've met Attractive Women who can discuss politics like they are Sunday morning talk show hosts and others who could discuss obscure trivia from *Star Trek*. These women are not cardboard cutouts. They are flesh and blood individuals who eat, sleep, and fart like everyone else.

The final piece of the puzzle I find most fascinating is that these women tend to be lonely. Yes, they do get plenty of date offers but they usually run into men who feel the need to flash money or play games. The men aren't thinking about the woman's intellectual ability or her personal interests. The woman's sexual needs may or may not be met yet she is consistently left high and dry as far as her emotional needs. The men trying to have sex with her don't care about her church activities or her comic book collection.

On the other hand, the Attractive Woman is not likely to have a lot of female friends. Women want attention from men.

This desire for attention makes women very competitive with each other as they will compete to get the most attention from the men in their environment. Plain and average women tend to dislike Attractive Women and are really the source of the negative stereotypes. As a consequence Attractive Women will tend to stay to themselves or if they are lucky hang out with other Attractive Women.

So for reference purposes, the profile of an Attractive Woman is someone who is physically beautiful, has a feminine persona, has varied personal interests, and tends to be a loner. It's important to keep this general profile in mind because it provides clues as to what a man needs to do to win the heart of one of these women. Please keep in mind, however, that these characteristics should not be considered absolute. Each Attractive Woman will have certain nuances unique to their personality.

Development Plan for Men

The key to establishing a relationship with an Attractive Woman is not knowing the right line, or simply projecting what a man thinks to be alpha male qualities. The key in any relationship is **compatibility**. Compatibility is the reason why any relationship succeeds or fails. It's why you occasionally see a very attractive woman with a dork. Looking from the outside it may seem like the dork used some type of game to get the woman. What is most likely is that the dork and the Attractive Woman have compatible personalities and interests to the extent that the woman ignored the dork's physical unattractiveness. Situations like this are rare, however, because in most cases the woman would put the dork into the "friend zone."

As an aside let me make one thing clear. A woman putting a man into the friend zone doesn't mean she doesn't want to get to know the man or she doesn't know a real man when she sees one. It means one thing and one thing alone. She and the man are compatible on a personality level but she does not find him physically attractive enough to have sex with him.

To date or have a relationship with an Attractive Woman the man must become compatible to her general profile. Now someone may think this means putting on a "front" but this is far from the case.

The one constant in the universe is change. Nothing stays the same. Not even the bodies we are in. A little known fact is that because of the death of cells we essentially have a new body every seven years. No matter where you are physically and mentally at this moment the potential for change is always there. All that's needed is the desire to change. If you are tired of being dateless or tired of dealing with unattractive women you need to make changes. The changes involve work. Forget about shortcuts like hypnotic patterns or pretending to be an alpha male. Women see through the lies immediately. The only way to get an Attractive Woman is to become her equal or better.

I previously provided a general profile of the Attractive Woman. I described her as being physically beautiful, feminine, having various interests and lonely. The man must develop his physical appearance, his masculine nature, pursue his interests, and start treating women differently. I wrote about these things in my previous books. Consider the following a different perspective on the issues I brought up.

Physical Appearance

A major portion of **Nice Guys and Players** and **Sexual Chemistry** focused on hitting the gym and dressing nicely. Unfortunately many men didn't see the practical purpose of this beyond aesthetics. First, let's look at this from the perspective of the Attractive Woman. She didn't get her looks and body sitting in her home playing video games and watching cable. The beautiful woman likely has a gym membership. She has spent many hours in aerobic classes and on weight machines. Her butt is so tight you could bounce a quarter off of it. Do you seriously think she wants a man who hasn't put as much effort into his body? She may deal with someone skinny or out of shape man for lack of better options. Rest assured, let a buffed man come into the picture and watch her reaction. There are, however, deeper aspects of physical appearance beyond that of mere aesthetics.

There are certain behaviors programmed into the DNA structure of every human being guaranteeing the survival of the species. One of those behaviors is the desire to procreate. Men and women are drawn together for this reason. Really think about it. When you see an Attractive Woman don't you feel a pulled to her like a magnet? You can feel it in your bones, in your very being. You're probably reading this book because you had this feeling and you couldn't act on it. To further facilitate this desire to procreate, within our DNA is a programmed body shape that is designed to make us optimally attractive to the opposite sex. For the woman the ideal shape is an hourglass figure with a contrast between the breasts, the waists, and the hips. This shape, when viewed by a man, will alter his body chemistry to prepare him for sexual intercourse. His adrenal glands will become more active. Blood will rush to his penis causing it to become erect, and his production of semen will increase.

Women have a similar response when they view certain indicators in men. The optimal shape which appeals to a woman is a V-shape. The man's chest should be slightly larger than his waist. When a man built this way is viewed by a woman her nipples will perk up and her body will become cold as the blood will rush to the region around her vagina causing her to become wet.

Now if we all had ideal body shapes there wouldn't be any problems with relationships. Unfortunately, though optimal mating is programmed into our DNA, humanity has found a way to screw it up.

From the time we are born our natural DNA programming comes under assault. Regarding sexuality we are constantly bombarded with messages that interfere with our natural sexual expression. One program is religion. Many organized religions associate sex with sin making it seem like it is something dirty and undesirable. Then you have other influences such as racism, classicism, and sexism, which have a distorting effect on our DNA programming to the point where it affects our physical appearance. For example, Denise is born into a strictly religious Black middle class family. The parents believe sex for other than procreation is wrong. The parents enforce this in the daughter every single day. In addition, though they are middle class they live in close proximity to a housing project where there are several people who are more lax in their sexual mores. On top of that the father is chauvinistic and believes that Black women are the cause of Black problems. So by the time the girl becomes an adult, she has an undeveloped body. Her breasts are very small, and her hips are like a man's with skinny shapeless legs. If her DNA programming were allowed free expression she would have developed an hourglass figure. Let's look at why she didn't.

First, Denise was brought up to believe that sex outside of marriage and procreation was wrong. This message entered her subconscious, which began making the changes to her programming as to her natural body shape. A woman with an hourglass shape would get too much attention to limit her sexuality to marriage and procreation. Second, classicism has an affect because her family felt like they were above the poorer people with whom they came in contact. These people, particularly the women, were more in line with their programming and thus closer to their ideal shapes. Denise consciously may not think anything about the poorer women's bodies but subconsciously she viewed having a shapely body as a bad thing. Racism and sexism put the final nails in the coffin. Denise's father feels like he has not accomplished some things in life because of a false belief that Black women are undermining him. Instead to trying to change the system or realizing that nobody has it easy he turns against his wife. Even though he was generally kind to Denise, she still felt subconsciously that being a shapely woman was a bad thing because her mother and most of the women her father seemed to hate were shapely. With all of these negative influences, the DNA programming in Denise became altered. Instead of a shapely, sexy woman you have a woman who is built like an adolescent male.

If a man is having trouble developing his physique he must take time out and become introspective. Being underweight or very overweight interferes with natural sexual attraction. This really has nothing to do with eating. That's why a skinny man can eat everything in sight and not put on a pound and a fat man can make a sincere effort at changing his eating habits and not lose any weight. Before engaging in a plan to develop the physique the man must examine his attitudes towards women. Many men, ironically men who call themselves nice guys, really don't like women. On the surface, they desire sex with women and normal interactions but subconsciously they may actually hate women. This could stem from a domineering mother, a neglectful mother, a first crush on a mean girl, constant rejection, or even in some cases incest. The man must deal with these issues in any way he can, be it therapy, or confronting the source of the issue. At the very least the man must make peace with the source of the issue and move on even if there are several other issues. Once this is done the skinny man will find that his weight will increase and the fat man will find that his weight will begin to come off easily.

So you've addressed your issues with the opposite sex and your physique becomes more muscular. Clothes and grooming become important at this point since no one can walk around buck-naked. Many take grooming and clothes for granted. In fact, one of the more interesting criticisms of **Nice Guys and Players** was my saying that men needed to dress well and clean themselves. There are deeper aspects of this. A man can groom himself well and wear nice clothes and still not come off as sexy to women. The reason lies with how the clothes are worn. People in society wear clothes in two general styles: as a magnifier and as a shield. Wearing clothes as a magnifier draws a person's attention to us in a sexual way. For example a shapely woman is walking down the street with a short mini-skirt, a cut-off top showing her belly ring, and four-inch pumps. She is using her clothes as a magnifier to draw attention to her in a sexual manner. Another woman with a similar body is walking down the street wearing a drab one-piece dress which goes down to her ankles, just above her flat shoes. She is using her clothes to deflect sexual attention from herself. The average man will not notice her. Both women are wearing clean clothes, however their different styles will have different affects on the men around them.

People can also groom themselves in a way that magnifies their sexuality or deflects attention. Using the above example, the woman dressed as a magnifier has loose wavy hair and tastefully applied makeup. Her grooming adds to her sex appeal. The woman dressed as a shield has straight hair tied in a bun, no makeup, and big glasses which obscures an otherwise beautiful face. Once again the average man will not give her a second look.

Even though the magnifier/shield dynamic can be applied more easily to women, men can also use this dynamic as well to enhance their sex appeal. With clothing a man must draw attention to himself in a sexual way. A man with a developed physique should wear shirts that are slightly loose, but form fitting to highlight his chest. Don't wear them too tight, as this can look cheesy unless you're going to a club. Pants should be slightly loose but form fitting as well. If you wear suits avoid anything off the rack. Always get a suit tailored to fit your physique. As far as dress shirts, slim fit is best. You want your clothing to highlight your body.

As far as grooming, staying clean is hopefully obvious. The key is what you do with your head. Women respond to handsome men, however being handsome isn't all about being born with a certain bone structure. Men born with facial bone structures appealing to a wide variety of women are rare. A man, however, can make himself handsome through grooming. Starting from the top and working down a man needs to work with his hair. Aside from regular shampoos and conditioning, a man should experiment with different looks to determine which look draws more attention from women. It's different for each man. For one man, it may mean letting his hair hang over his forehead while for another his hair looks best brushed back. Yet another man may look best with a shaved head. When you find the look that works best go with it.

Next are the eyes. Women consider eyes to be very sexy. Sometimes this has to do with the eye color such as ice blue or green. Sometimes it has to do with the shape such as having almond eyes if one is not Asian. If you have regular eyes there are still things you can do to make them more attractive. One thing is to get more rest. Most people have blood shot eyes because they don't get enough sleep. Also leave alcohol and other drugs alone and work on any internal health problems. A person's eyes provide clues to a person's internal health. Subconsciously, this is one reason why a woman likes to look into a man's eyes; she can get an indication of his state of health.

Many men wear glasses. As with hair, experiment with different looks. If women respond more to you without glasses, invest in contacts. If you don't want contacts, shop for a pair of glasses that better fit your face. Many women like men with glasses. Moving on down, determine whether women like you better with facial hair or without. Sometimes facial hair preferences indicate a woman's social class. Women from more middle to upper class backgrounds tend to like clean-shaven looks while women from more lower class backgrounds tend to like men with facial hair, particularly moustaches.

Finally the teeth. White and straight is universally admired as far as teeth. Make the dentist a valued friend. If your teeth are jacked up, you need to invest in them more than trying to impress women with your bankroll.

By developing your physical appearance now you have something in common with the Attractive Woman. She's physically attractive and now you're physically attractive. A law of the universe is that like attracts like. If you walk into a club, or just down the street, an Attractive Woman will notice a very attractive man. She will be more receptive to your approach and since you both are in great shape you can establish an immediate connection because it will be obvious that you both work out. You have an opening and a conversation piece. The physical appearance is the first part of the puzzle as more is needed to truly connect with the Attractive Woman.

Masculine Sensuality

You have identical twin men who are very good-looking with killer physiques and sharp clothes. Despite being physically similar women would rate one twin a seven and the other twin is a ten. Why? The seven is very emotional, indecisive, and behaves like a teenager at times. The ten, on the other hand, is always calm, keeps a serious look on his face, and is very mature. Women may respond to the seven because of his looks but will soon lose interest because of his behavior. Women will not only respond to the ten but will fall in love with him.

Attractive Women have developed their feminine sensuality to its highest level. Their very aura projects sensuality. A woman with this type of sensuality is not going to respond well to a man saying canned lines, flashing money, or even in a few rare cases a man with a great body. These women will respond most strongly to raw masculine sensuality.

Both **Nice Guys and Players** and **Sexual Chemistry** provided ways to develop raw sensuality and it will serve the reader well to refer to the books. For purposes of this discussion I want to focus more on the primal nature of male sensuality.

As stated earlier our DNA carries certain programs necessary for the survival of the species, primary of which is the desire to procreate. Now obviously this desire manifests differently in women and men. Women procreate in their wombs after having their eggs fertilized by sperm received from men. Think about this for a second. A woman gets pregnant only after RECEIVING sperm from a man. A woman's eggs cannot leave her body, go get fertilized by sperm, and then come back. The only way a woman gets pregnant is by receiving sperm. To facilitate this process the DNA carries programs that cause a female to have attributes that will DRAW men to her. Physically, this is a shapely figure. This shapely figure is enhanced by attitudes that encourage the man to approach the woman. These attitudes are generally receptivity and passivity. The DNA causes a woman to behave in a manner that makes it easier for a man to approach her and deposit his seed. Most women don't realize it but they stay healthy when they behave in a more passive and receptive manner. Women's bodies are not built for more aggressive activities. Many women have health problems because they are engaged in activities more suited to men. This is not sexist. Anybody with eyes can see that men and women are built differently and thus are more suited to certain activities.

Now the same DNA, which causes a woman to be shapely and receptive, also causes a man to be muscular and aggressive. A woman's eggs are not going to come to the man. The only way a man is going to procreate is to find a woman who is receptive to receiving his seed. This manifests in the man's overall persona by making him assertive and aggressive in his daily life. This is the man who will actively pursue the things he desires. If he wants material goods he will actively take the steps to acquire these goods. If he wants a woman he will actively pursue women. A man expressing his natural sensuality will be a man of action. He will not be passive in the face of life.

Now here's where developing your physique becomes very important. Many men don't want to join a gym, and feel like this isn't important. Yet these same men want to be more masculine. Let me drop some knowledge on you. Raw masculinity at the most primal level is pure aggression. In the wild it's the predator. In more civilized environments it's the man who takes action. A man, however, really can't take much action if he has a skinny weak body or an overweight body which tires out after a little exertion. A man has to **PHYSICALLY** be able to take action. Action isn't an intellectual thing where a man talks about what he's going to do. Many men call themselves real men because they are good citizens. That's some bullshit. Many men are good citizens because they don't have the physical ability to go against the grain. Sometimes the action a man takes may require that he smack the shit out of another man. He can't do this if he doesn't have the physical strength to carry out this action.

Bottom line, every man needs to engage in a physical training program. Forget the aesthetics. You want to have the strength to take action.

Okay so now you've got into your body. All of a sudden you notice that you're becoming more aggressive. Your body, in response to the demands placed on it by weight training, will increase the production of testosterone, the hormone that makes men aggressive. You're no way as patient as you used to be. You feel more of an urge to smack a man for making a snide remark. You feel a strong urge to grab the sexy woman you see walking down the street, take her in an alley, and bang the shit out of her. At a primal level this is raw maleness. More is needed, however, to make a man sensual. In my books I stated that a man must make a woman comfortable to arouse her sexually. The woman is not going to be comfortable if she feels like the man is going to beat and rape her. The woman is responding to the raw maleness on one level but on another level she is turned off, as she may fear for her safety. For a man to be truly sensual he must have full control over his primal male energy. The key to this is for the man to develop a disciplined nature.

One of the most talked about issues in male-female relationships is the subject of good girls and bad boys. The reason good girls fall for bad boys is the sensuality projected by these men. These men, be they rock star, pro athlete, or drug dealer are connected with their primal maleness. This alone sets them apart from most men. To make it in any profession be it music, sports, or illegal activity, a man has to have control over his primal instincts. Rock stars, no matter how crazy they act, have to practice their music and deal with business matters. Pro athletes have to practice many hours because they may be cut from the team for making a costly mistake during the game. Drug dealers have to be very disciplined or they wind up in jail or dead. Applied to interactions with women, the man is turning the women on by his primal maleness but his disciplined nature keeps his primal maleness from harming her.

In indigenous societies, past and present, a man wasn't considered a man until he successfully completed a rites of passage. The primary purpose of these rites of passage was to teach a man how to control his primal nature. One of the reasons there is so much crime, violence, and rape rampant in this society is because there are no formal rites of passage for the majority of boys. Indeed warrior codes were developed in past societies to provide a man with the means to control his nature.

For a man to develop his full male sensuality he must first develop his body and then a personal code to live by. This code can come from religion, a philosophy, or the social mores of the particular region where you live. This code must be personalized to your needs. Each individual is different and what one person may need to do to control his primal nature may not be as effective for the next person. This code has to be something that YOU enforce. Too often people behave in certain ways because of outside influences. Most people refuse to rob and steal not because it's wrong to take somebody's property but because they are afraid of the penalty society would inflict on them if caught. Self-regulation contributes to a man's sensuality. Another aspect of a man's primal maleness is the desire to control his environment. Men are most comfortable when they have their own means of income and when his family and associates look to him for leadership. The only thing a man can establish 100% control over is himself. The greatest control a man can have is over his sex drive. If a man can control and harness this drive there is nothing he cannot accomplish.

  For the man reading this I suggest writing a set of rules to follow for dealing with women. After following these rules for a while you will find that these rules will become embedded in your subconscious to the point you follow them without consciously thinking about your actions. In my player days I had a code I lived by in my interactions with women. One, I didn't have sex with married women even though they showed interest. I only dealt with women with boyfriends if <u>they</u> were persistent and I eventually got to the point where I wouldn't mess with them. Turns out, women started lying about their relationship status, but that's another book. I would never have sex with a drunk woman. I never hung out with a woman as "just friends." If all I wanted from a woman was sex I told her upfront even if this meant I would lose a chance with her. Following this code meant that I had less drama than the average man. Women knew where they stood with me and thus were more comfortable with me even though they considered me a player. My code allowed me to keep my sex drive under control.

True male sensuality can be described as "controlled ferocity." A man with controlled ferocity projects a power which women find appealing. The keys are developing the body and living by a code of honor to control the primal nature.

Gift of Gab

Okay so now you have a killer physique, and you're reeking of raw masculinity. At this point you're going to get a lot of attention from women and a lot of short term relationships based on lustful mutual attraction. Funny thing is that rarely will this type of man hook up with the Attractive Woman. She thinks you're sexy but this alone will not cause her to have sex with you. It's very easy for a sexy man to get sex from women who are more average in appearance. All the man has to do is show even a little interest. Average-looking women rarely get an opportunity to get with a physically desirable man. When they do they are quick to take advantage. This is a dynamic in which male exotic dancers take full advantage. Now an Attractive Woman has a different mindset because she usually has physically desirable men hitting on her on a consistent basis. She will tend to be more patient about getting into a relationship. With so many men hitting on them they will develop a tendency to look beyond physical appearance. Don't get it twisted; they will never ignore the physical package. The Attractive Woman is simply looking for more substance.

In the profile for the Attractive Woman I pointed out that she will have a range of interests. Even the women who initially come off as airheads are deeper once you find out what really interests them. The key is the ability to be compatible with their interests. So if a woman is interested in the history of dandelions, you can have an effective conversation with her even though to you dandelions are just weeds that mess up a perfectly good lawn. Old school players call this the "Gift of Gab." The gift of gab is simply the ability to talk with anyone about anything and to be comfortable in any situation. A man with the gift of gab will not have any problems getting women because he will always have the ability to develop a rapport with a woman.

Developing the Gift of Gab is extremely difficult but can be done. Just don't expect overnight results. For example, I can state without conceit that I have the gift of gab. This took a lifetime to develop as I have been exposed to a variety of people and situations. I can hang with the fellas on the corner of a housing project in the morning and then attend a formal dinner with the most powerful people in the world in the evening. For the man reading this don't expect to get to that particular level in this lifetime. I'm just keeping it real. At the same time the number of men who got it like that represents maybe 10% of the human male population. This means you can WORK to develop the gift and improve from wherever you are now. You may potentially be a part of that 10% and not realize your buried gift. There are two steps that must be taken to develop the gift. First, you must develop an open mind. Second, a man must develop his interests.

Most people are closed-minded. This closed-mindedness limits the life experience of a person. He will be afraid to explore new things and new people. The more closed-minded a person is the more stuck he will be in negative situations. Regarding the Attractive Woman, many men have preconceived notions as to her personality and interests. For example, many so-called pick-up artists assume that an Attractive Woman is an airhead who has nothing to do but look good. They also assume that a canned routine will work on these women based on stereotypes. Here's the problem: these women have personalities and interests. Most pick-up artists get thrown off when the woman exhibits a trait or action not discussed on a message board or workshop.

A man has to be open to all possibilities when dealing with any woman. You might approach an Attractive Woman who appears to be an airhead but instead find out she is a corporate executive. I had a lady friend who dressed like an exotic dancer and yet was pursuing a doctorate. You have to be open to any and all possibilities.

A key ingredient to being open-minded is the willingness to learn something new from any source. Many people are closed-minded in this regard because they feel that they can learn only from certain people in certain situations. For example I'm aware of a few people who rejected the information in **Nice Guys and Players** because I'm not a PhD in Psychology. They refused to utilize the advice. Someone more open-minded will read the information, apply it, and if they didn't get results then they will reject the information. If they got results they will accept the information. Regarding the Attractive Woman, the man must be open to learning something from her. That way no matter what she talks about it will add to your knowledge.

Being open to new things means that you will take a sincere interest in what the woman is talking about. Every single person on the planet wants to feel like his or her viewpoint is being heard. I believe that's the reason Internet message boards are so popular. Message boards allow people to really say what's on their minds without having to face a major repercussion. A weak man on a message board can talk trash and even threaten people with bodily harm because he is simply a screenname. The same man would get his ass kicked if he did the same thing at a shopping mall. All people want to be heard and be considered interesting. An Attractive Woman wants to be seen as interesting beyond her looks. Here's a bit of wisdom to employ when talking with such a woman. When she's talking look at her the same way you would if an ugly woman was doing the talking. If someone is communicating something of interest to you, you going to be focused more on the subject than her beautiful eyes. This impresses her as she is used to men staring at her with puppy dog eyes.

Now you're open to new things. You have become someone that others can learn from. One thing I find fascinating about women regardless of their physical appearance: they are willing to listen to a man who is communicating information in an intelligent manner. Put another way they like men who have good conversation skills. A man has to have something to talk about. One problem many men have is that the subjects they can talk about are so limited. For example a man's interests may be focused on political issues. If he meets a woman whose interests are political as well there will be a connection. In all likelihood though, the woman will not have the same interests. A man has to be able to communicate a subject that is of interest to the woman. It's impossible for a man to learn about everything to the point of being able to talk about everything. He can however, get an idea about what is important to the average woman.

In addition, a man should pursue interests in different areas just to become a better person. The key to success in life is the ability to meet different challenges. Every experience we have in life is something we can call upon when presented with a challenge. For example, in college I hustled gigs for a DJ friend of mine and even helped him spin records. Years later when I started setting up workshops for people those same skills came into play when it came time to make a living. On another level by doing and experiencing different things I had a variety of things to talk about with different women. Woman generally like a man who has lived an interesting life.

Get out and just live. Experience new things. If you work in an office, take a part-time job doing manual labor. If you work as a deliveryman, develop a book collection. Get out of your comfort zone. Take different routes to work. Eat at restaurants serving food foreign to your culture. Go where you can interact with people of different cultures. Expand your mind. As you do this you will become more interesting to the women you meet.

One final thing with the gift of gab. I'm sure plenty of people reading this are thinking about how shy they are and that they would like techniques to get over this shyness. Well if a man develops his physique, gets in touch with his inner masculinity, and then works on opening his mind and developing different interests he will get over any shyness. He will **naturally** become more assertive. There is one more piece to the puzzle for the man who wants to meet and date Attractive women. It's being a gentleman.

Be a Gentleman

This is a quote from a man who embodies the principles contained in this book.

> That's where we get into the importance of being a gentleman. Believe it or not, old-fashioned concepts of chivalry & etiquette are the most proven form of productive interaction between men and women. It's considerate, gentle and kind. It separates the boys from the real men. Many of these cats today can't or refuse to recognize the significance of this. The laws of the universe dictate that the female expects and deserves gentle treatment even during times of conflict. That's lacking in today's society. Which is why most women that I'll hold the door open for will suddenly get weak in the knees and feel as though it's love at first sight. Or, they think that I'm trying to make a move on them. But, I'm not doing either. I'm simply fulfilling my obligation to the laws of the universe and what God intended. Being a

gentleman is a natural component of the male personality. It is a discipline that should be taught from pre-school.

See there is this fucked-up perception that being a gentleman is being weak. But, let me school you for a moment. Some of the hardest, most lethal, most effective warriors in history were the most romantic and passionate men to ever walk the face of the Earth. The famous WWII General Patton wrote eloquent poetry while he was crushing Hitler's Nazis. Samurais in Japan were recognized for their etiquette than they were for swordsmanship.

One problem I see with many dating and seduction manuals is that they seem to give the impression that being an "alpha male" is only about being tough, in charge, cocky and funny, and basically an all around bad-ass towards women. This is someone wearing the mask of what they believe to be an alpha male. If you look at alpha males in the animal kingdom whether it's the Lion Pride, Wolf Pack, or Gorilla Clan, the alpha males are quite gentle towards the females and cubs. It's against threats to the group the alpha male becomes vicious. In human society, some of the deadliest gangsters are soft and gentle when dealing with their women and children.

Many nice guys who have been constantly passed over are reading this wondering what have they done wrong since they are always gentlemen. The problem with the nice guy is that they tend to be passive in other areas of life. Women want to see their men kick ass in life. Women want to feel proud of their men. How can a woman feel proud or even respect a man who isn't truly making his mark in life? Another problem with the nice guy is that his niceness doesn't come off as sincere. Many women feel like a man is being nice to them as simply a tactic to get sex. Indeed with many men it is a tactic. Yet another issue with the nice guy is that he will tolerate poor treatment from a woman because he believes this is the gentlemanly thing to do. That's some bullshit. If a woman is being disrespectful you can still put her in check in a gentlemanly fashion. For example, if a woman was to step to me in a harsh manner. I would just look at her and say in a calm, cool respectful way, "Miss, I'm not sure what you think of me but I'm not a person to play with. If you have a problem with me we can discuss it like adults." Ninety-nine percent of the time this will calm them down.

Now there are plenty of women who don't respond to gentlemanly behavior even when it comes from an otherwise sexy man. LEAVE THESE WOMEN ALONE!!! A gentleman wants a LADY. He wants someone who is the personification of beauty and class. This is what makes ANY woman attractive. A truly Attractive Woman is a lady who will demand respect. Women who respond to mistreatment have issues. A man who is about something shouldn't even think about sticking his dick in one of these women. I know these women are sexy but if she lets you get away with treating her poorly rest assured it will come back and bite you. That's one thing I see with nice guys: too many of them are chasing hoes only because they are physically attractive. An Attractive Woman is beautiful inside and out.

In the profile of the Attractive Woman I stated that they tended to be lonely. These women catch hell from all corners. Many of them need somebody to be genuinely kind to them. Many of them need a real friend and not somebody with an ulterior motive. These women respond very well to real gentlemen.

Look, I know men who read these types of books look for steps to take to accomplish a certain goal or state. If I have to tell a grown ass man HOW to be a gentleman there's some issues he needs to deal with that go beyond what I could tell you in a book. There are some things a man SHOULD know. All I'm really saying is that it's okay to be a gentleman. The key is simply to balance it out with a backbone. Treat all women with kindness and respect but have zero tolerance for bad treatment.

Erotic Aura

You have developed your physical appearance, your masculine persona, the gift of gab, and are behaving like a gentleman. The combination of sensuality and manners in a man makes him a charmer. Think for a second about an Attractive Woman who is very nice. You see this very beautiful and sexy woman walking towards you in the street or a bar. You think she will ignore you but instead she starts talking to you in a flirty manner. At that moment she can get you to do anything she wants. She's a charmer.

A defining feature of a charmer is his sex appeal. When a charmer meets a woman, his sex appeal puts her into a relaxed state in which she not so much lowers her defenses, but subconsciously

WANTS to lower her defenses. The average man, however, not realizing that the woman finds him sexy will start running different lines and use other equally stupid tactics which turn the woman off. The charmer realizes that if a woman finds him sexy, it's easier to get her to lower her defenses if he is NICE to her. One catches more flies with honey than with vinegar. What the charmer has is an erotic aura.

Everyone has an aura. The word "aura" is thrown around a lot in metaphysic circles, usually in relation to subtle electro-magnetic energy that surrounds the human body. Another way to look at the aura is the non-verbal presentation one makes to the people around them. For example, a man tells you he has slept with ten women in the past month. He sounds convincing as he tells you the lines he used and the details of each encounter. While he is telling you this you mentally note that he is ugly, overweight, poorly dressed, and is obnoxious. A part of you wants to believe him because it gives you hope than an "ordinary" guy can get laid, but in the back of your mind you wonder how could he possibly be appealing to women since his aura suggests that they wouldn't find him attractive.

Another example is when a man tells you he hasn't slept with a woman in two years. You immediately think he is lying or gay despite how sincere he sounds. The man is handsome, masculine, dresses well and has money; the image suggests that he wouldn't have any problem getting a woman.

Only seven percent of communication between two people is verbal and conscious. Thus ninety three percent of communication is non-verbal and subconscious. Obviously the subconscious/non-verbal communication will carry more weight. Most relationships fail because people are not compatible on a subconscious level. To the greatest extent possible you want to strive for subconscious compatibility. Looking at the traits of Attractive Women and the development plan I presented we can see how a man can achieve this compatibility. The Attractive Woman is obviously physically beautiful with a shapely body, which means she values good health and appearance. If she values this in herself she will value it in a man. Beautiful women may go out with average men but deep down they would like more attractive men. On a primal level if a woman has an optimal shape that draws men to her, she will want a man with an optimal shape.

The Attractive Woman is in touch with her feminine sensuality, thus she is not going to want a man who isn't truly masculine. Many men put on a masculine façade that crumbles as soon as a crisis occurs. Subconsciously a woman wouldn't feel a strong attraction to this man even though consciously she finds him attractive. She may feel slightly repulsed by a man faking masculinity. Think of two magnets with negative polarities. They will repel each other. Now a magnet with a positive polarity and one with a negative polarity will draw together. Think of a masculine man having a positive polarity while a feminine woman having a negative polarity. This dynamic must be present in order for a relationship to have real chance for success.

A woman with various interests will instinctively look for a man who is interesting himself or at the very least open to new things.

Finally, a truly Attractive Woman will behave like a true lady. Regardless of how the man may behave towards other people the woman will expect gentlemanly treatment from him.

Here's some wisdom. People are most strongly attracted to those who reflect what they think about themselves. Every person who thinks highly of himself or herself wants to see their reflection in their mates. Often you read and hear about beautiful women who are with ugly, out of shape losers. These women, when you actually see them, probably have issues they need to deal with. Consider a statement made by a character in Ayn Rand's classic novel, **Atlas Shrugged**:

> Tell me what a man finds sexually attractive and I will tell you his entire philosophy of life. Show me the woman he sleeps with and I will tell you his valuation of himself...
>
> He will always be attracted to the woman who reflects his deepest vision of himself, the woman whose surrender permits him to experience - or to fake - a sense of self-esteem. The man who is proudly certain of his own value, will want the highest type of woman he can find, the woman he admires, the strongest, the hardest to conquer -because only the possession of a heroine will give him the sense of an achievement, not the possession of a brainless slut.
>
> Page 455

****

A woman will always want a man who reflects her. That's the whole point of a man developing himself. This development can't hinge on canned routines. Women can see through that. A man has to have an aura that reflects the values of the Super-Attractive Woman. The more a man doesn't reflect the woman's values with his aura the more trouble he will have trying to date her.

Meeting Attractive Women Made Simple

Okay now it's time to present my methods for meeting women. Developing an erotic aura is the first step. The second step is to realize that women choose the men as explained in my previous books. (For a deeper understanding of how women choose please see appendix.) Men still have to approach the woman once she indicates an interest. This subconsciously tells the woman that you are aggressive and assertive. For whatever reason, men who are lions in other areas of life become pussycats when it comes to women. Quite frankly they are scared to approach women. This stems from a fear of rejection. Before a man can focus on meeting women he must focus on overcoming this fear. There are several ways in which this can be done.

Overcoming the Fear of Rejection

I recall one person who said that my books focused a lot on the body. That's because the body is the vehicle through which we take any type of action. Also by developing the body you develop the means to combat fear because you can withstand the pain of rejection.

Rejection can cause physical pain. For example when a man was a teenager he had a crush on the most beautiful girl in school. He would get excited everytime he saw her. He could actually feel it in his body. He got the nerve to approach the girl and she rejected him in a harsh and cruel manner. The boy is in pain. This happened with other beautiful girls as well. His subconscious tells him that these beautiful women can hurt him by rejecting him so he begins to deal with less attractive women though a part of him will always want the beautiful ones.

The human body has a fight or flight response to perceived danger. A man constantly rejected by beautiful women will perceive them as dangerous and will get nervous around them and will have an urge to run away. This fear is why many men try to control women, play games, and even hate them. Even when men are in relationships with attractive women there are many fear based issues such as, 1) being controlling – what you control can't hurt you, 2) being clingy – what you cling to can't leave you, or 3) being a pushover because they feel that the woman may leave if they stand their ground. These men are affected by the fight or flight response thus developing coping strategies to deal with their pain.

In developing your body you slowly develop the ability to face your fears. One of the biggest fears a man will have to face is whether he can physically handle himself in a physical confrontation. Men don't talk about it but we all know it's there. Men fear physical harm at the hands of another man more than anything else. By developing your body, particularly through strength training you will begin to feel like you can handle yourself in a fight. Once you conquer the fear of physical harm, other fears will begin to disappear. Another thing you want to do is take up a martial art that requires contact sparring or playing in a football league where physical hitting is permitted. Once you lose the fear of pain, the physical fear reaction to a beautiful woman will begin to disappear. The bottom line is to face your fears. If you are scared of flying, take a long flight to anywhere. If you are scared of heights, go hang out on the rooftop of a tall building. FACE YOUR FEARS!!!

Regarding Attractive Women there are specific steps you can take to overcome your fear of rejection.

The first thing a man must do to get over his fear of rejection by an Attractive Woman is to get used to talking to women on a consistent basis. Starting today randomly speak to women who cross your path. Keep it very simple. Say "Hi" or "How are you doing today?" In most cases don't take it further. If you are in a checkout line at a supermarket or retail store always say "thank you", and "have a nice day." This seems simple but by doing these things you gradually get used to speaking to different women. Thus when you run into a woman you want to get to know romantically you can speak to her without fear or hesitation.

Now you can speak to women without hesitation but you still need something to talk about. Most men have some type of female acquaintance whether a neighbor, a co-worker or even a family member. Just start talking to them more about anything. Develop the habit of getting into conversations where your intention is **NOT** to get laid. Here's a page from Rom's old player book from back in the day. When I talked to women I was interested in, my conversations were rarely flirtatious. I would talk about ordinary things. I also had regular conversations with co-workers, female friends, and sometimes strangers on the bus. Though women like romantic talk and flirting with men they can just as stimulated by a man talking about subjects he's passionate about. One of the biggest complaints women have is that many men have lousy conversation skills. Many women will reject a physically appealing man because he can't hold a conversation. Let me school you for a second. A man can go anywhere in the world and have a conversation with another man about women or sports. With women you can always have a conversation about relationships. Always remember this.

An extreme method of getting over the fear of rejection is to go to a club and look for the most beautiful woman who <u>also</u> seems like she's the harshest. Look for a woman who has been rejecting men all night. For a week beforehand think about nothing else but going to a club to find the most beautiful woman that will likely reject you. When you get to the club order a drink and just observe. When you spot the woman walk over to her and ask her to dance. If she says "no" with an attitude, look at her and say with a smile, "I'm sorry for disturbing you. I hope you enjoy your evening." Now pay attention to how you feel at that moment. A physically attractive woman has just rejected you and instead of getting upset you are polite to her. Your subconscious starts thinking, "You know, rejection is bad only when I get upset. When I'm cool with it, I'm not bothered." Once a rude woman rejects a man harshly, no other rejection will make you lose your inner cool.

There's one additional method that a man can employ to get over his fear of rejection. As stated earlier a man's fear of a beautiful woman stems from the possibility of rejection. From a personal viewpoint I never had a fear of rejection because a stronger urge in my consciousness was my desire for pleasure. When I saw a beautiful, sexy woman my first thought was not that she would reject me. My first thought was an image of her legs wrapped around my back. Pure lust overcame the fear instinct to the point where for me approaching a beautiful woman was the most natural thing in the world. Let me tell you a small tidbit about me. I didn't have a notion that sex was considered a sin until I attended a Catholic High School. As result where most people had been conditioned to repress their desires mine were fairly out of control. Therefore I had no problems interacting with women even though I still had lot to learn as far as getting them to bed. My problem was that I was overly aggressive to the point of being crude. I wasn't a smooth operator. I became more attractive to women once I learned to manage my sex drive.

Focus more on pleasure. Let's be real, when you initially approach a woman you're thinking about sex with her. Don't lie to yourself. The woman knows why you're approaching. Just do it as gentleman and talk to her to find where her interests are. If she likes you she'll allow matters to progress. Don't suppress your lust, harness it and ride it like a horse to its destination. Trust me when you <u>really</u> want a woman, you will find the courage you didn't think you had.

Let me leave this section with a true story. When I was in law school there was young lady who played on the undergrad women's basketball team. She was a very hard worker and good player. Her teammates and everybody who saw her play thought so. Apparently her coach didn't share everyone's opinion. The young lady would get maybe two minutes of playing time and in that period would get three rebounds, a blocked shot, a steal, and a basket. Then the coach would take her out. It was becoming a controversial situation. Everybody seemed upset EXCEPT the young lady. She kept her spirits up and would even make excuses for why the coach wouldn't play her. Anyway one day I was walking through the school gym when I saw her shooting free throws by herself. I walked over to her and expressed my sympathy for her situation and made a comment about her practicing by herself. She said something that always stuck with me. She said, "Rom, I'm going to make it so that they CAN'T take me out the game." She was a sophomore when she said this. Not only was she starting by her senior year, she also made the all-league team.

For the man who has been constantly rejected, work until you get to the point where a woman CAN'T reject you.

Approaching and Meeting Women

I recommend four primary ways of approaching and meeting women. They are referred to as Slow Walk, Quick Strike, Friend Zone, and Dance Hall.

Slow Walk

Slow walk is best utilized in situations where you know you'll consistently see a particular woman. Examples of this are women who work in retail stores and banks. Also this method is best utilized when you see a woman consistently at a bus stop, in your office building, at the gym, or even at the grocery store, or nightclub. The key with Slow Walk is to enter her world slowly.

The first step is to put yourself in a position where she can see you first. You can do this by walking past her without looking at her. In this way you are becoming a part of the scenery of her landscape. She may initially be unaware of your presence but will soon become aware. Starting this way does two things. First it allows the woman a chance to inspect you and if she likes what she sees she will begin to put herself in a position for you to approach. She may even approach you first, though a man shouldn't count on this happening. Second, starting off this way allows the woman to become comfortable with your presence. Most women are defensive around men they don't know. You want the woman to have her defenses lowered when you decide to approach. Even if the woman finds you attractive, if her defenses are up, an initial meeting may be difficult. You want her to be as comfortable as possible. After letting her see you around for a week or two, position yourself to cross her path. If she works as a retail clerk, buy something from her, but don't try to start a conversation unless she initiates it. A beautiful woman working as a clerk has several men hitting on her everyday. You'll stand out more by not trying to talk to her. Get in her line a few more times and she'll probably start a conversation with you. In a situation where you always see a woman in the same spot everyday like a bus stop or office building, initially say "hi" a couple of times and then maybe "How are you today?" If she doesn't respond at this point leave her alone. Most women, however, will be responsive.

Don't think in terms of getting her phone number at this point. You really don't need it since you talk to her everyday or so anyway. Now once you feel she's comfortable with you and most importantly **YOU** feel comfortable with her, get her phone number and set up a date.

Using Slow Walk allows the woman to check you out and get comfortable. It also makes you stand out because most men are too aggressive with women. Most women appreciate a man who takes his time. It subtly gives them the impression that you will take your time in the bedroom as well. It also gives her a chance to choose you and make it easier for you to approach her.

Slow Walk also gives you a chance to check her out. Men who are doing something with their lives are choosy about the women they will approach. A smart man looks for quality over quantity. Many woman look good on the surface but underneath are mean and cold. Check out the woman until you determine that she is beautiful inside as well as outside.

Slow Walk in my opinion is the best method of interaction between a man and woman. A woman gets to inspect and choose the man. A man can check out a woman to determine if she meets his standards.

Quick Strike

The Quick Strike is used only in two situations. The first is when a woman is being unusually aggressive or being obvious that she wants you to approach her. If she is appealing, you can date her easily. The key in this regard is not to blow it by thinking too much. The average man blows it with a woman because he thinks about his game plan and ends up hesitating because of second-guessing. When a woman is making her intentions obvious all a man really needs to do is say "hi" and nod his head. An aggressive woman will do most of the talking.

The second instance in which to employ a Quick Strike is when a woman is so fine, you know you'll kick yourself for weeks afterwards if you didn't try to meet her. In this case it's better to approach and get rejected than to not approach and have regrets.

Generally, I advise against doing cold approaches. You don't get a chance to check her out. You should be focused on other things if you are out in public. Also if you are ready to hit on her, at least five other men have already done so thus she may not be receptive. With all that said sometimes you will run into a woman so attractive that you want to get down on the ground and make love to her shadow. In this case I advise using the "Damn principle."

The "Damn Principle" is a situation when a woman is so beautiful, so gorgeous that you look at her and the first word out of your mouth is "damn" or something similar in tone. In this case approach as quickly as possible. You want to approach quicker than normal because your reaction will be more natural and spontaneous. If you stop and think in terms of lines and canned approaches, you may come off as nervous or like an obvious player. You want to come off like you don't approach women on the street on a consistent basis. The men who are most desirable to women typically don't do cold approaches. When was the last time you have seen a corporate executive or a pretty boy approach a woman on the street? When you appear like you don't do cold approaches regularly the woman will feel a bit special because she got a man to do something he doesn't do normally. By making her feel special you have a stronger likelihood of getting her phone number and whatever else you want from her.

Save the Quick Strike for special occasions.

The Friend Zone

Most men complain about the dreaded "friend zone." You know those hated words, "let's be friends." Now how is this a method to meet women? Easily, just pay attention. First, if a woman puts you into the "friend zone," don't get mad or show a reaction. Just accept it and treat her like a friend. Start asking her advice on other women. She can give you advice and insight about women that you can't get from another man. She can tell you what you need to do to become more attractive. She can tell you what buttons can be pushed on a particular woman.

The most important thing you get from the woman is an introduction to her friends. Women tend to be more comfortable with a man introduced to them by someone they know. Also you may be more compatible with one of her friends.

The key with this is to suppress any feelings you have for the woman friend. Though difficult, forget how sexy she is, and recall the time you saw her without her hair fixed or the time she farted in your car. In your mind she will truly become your friend.

Now an interesting thing happens when a woman becomes your friend. The woman will basically give you advice on what SHE likes in a man. If you follow it, you will gradually become the man who is closest to her ideal. Also as you start to show interest in other women, the woman friend will eventually notice your lack of attention and will do what she can to get it back. The woman friend will especially fight to win back your attention if your new woman is very attractive. All of a sudden the woman will rethink the whole platonic thing.

Another way to work the Friend Zone is to put attractive women there yourself. Women, regardless of their physical appearance and social standing, expect a man to try to get sex from them. It throws a woman off-balance if you only want to be friends with her and you aren't married or gay. It makes her work harder for your attention because if she can't get you to desire her sexually it messes with her self-esteem. Ironically she might think you're the ugliest loser on the planet but she'll try to give you some booty to make herself feel good. Putting women in the Friend Zone lets them know that you have better things to do than to get in their panties. It lets her know that you have self-discipline, which is a key masculine trait. It lets her know that you have certain standards which she will have to meet.

An important aspect of putting women into the Friend Zone is that you can keep a lot of women around without having to date them and dealing with the drama that comes with that. If you aren't around when a woman called five times in one night she can't get mad because you and she are "just friends."

Finally Friend Zone gives you a chance to get to know a woman. You might meet a woman and at first she seems like she has it going on. Then as you get to know her you find out she is a shady person. Too many men will have sex with any available woman. Then men get mad when they get a burning sensation while urinating, or she tells you her period is late, or worse you take a routine blood test and the doctor says he needs to see you in his office right away.

Use the Friend Zone to get to know women and to weed out undesirables.

Dance Hall

The best place to meet a woman hands down is a dance club. Not a bar but a dance club. Remember these words: **women love to dance.** The dance club is the one place where a normally defensive woman will be more receptive. It's the one place where it's okay for her to be sexual and wear that low cut black dress she keeps in the back of her closet. Despite how receptive woman are at clubs many men act like it takes rocket science to meet these women. It used to amaze me how men would stand around posing with drinks while women, using body language, were damn near begging the men to approach them.

One problem is that most men can't dance and most seduction message boards focus more on interactions in bars than in dance clubs. Let me let you in on something: Rom is not a great dancer. Yet I've lost count of how many women I got phone numbers and other things from after dancing with them. Why? Despite having trouble finding the beat I had fun!!! I didn't go out there to win a dance contest. I only wanted to dance with a nice woman. Most of the time I would click with woman. Sometimes it would be "thanks for the dance", and I would be off to find a new partner. If you are not a great dancer, who cares? Have a good time.

I had a specific method for meeting a woman in a dance club. First I would get to the club and relax a bit. I would get a drink for myself and a feel for the energy of the place. After getting a feel for the place I would look for two things. One, a woman standing by the dance floor moving to the music, or two, a woman sitting in her seat moving to the music. If a woman was doing neither I would only approach using the Damn Principle. Once I decided on a dance partner I would approach her and say, "May I have this dance?" If she said "no" I would say, "thank you anyway" and relax a bit before looking for another dance partner. Never look for another partner immediately after a rejection. You don't want to look like you will just dance with anyone to the other women checking you out.

In most cases the woman will say "yes." Take her out on the dance floor and start dancing. Don't try to talk to her out there because in most cases you'll be screaming over the music. At this point it's about body language. Pay attention to HOW she is dancing. If there is space between the two of you and she hardly looks at you, thank her for the dance after the song is over and relax a bit before looking for a new partner. If she is looking at you and getting close to you and continues dancing after the song goes off and another comes on, she is receptive to talking with you after leaving the dance floor. If the DJ puts on a slow song ask her for a slow dance. Women who slow dance with a stranger are interested in getting to know that stranger. A man can only blow it at this point.

By dancing with the woman first your bodies will make a determination as to compatibility. Remember, ninety-three percent of communication is subconscious. Many women respond to a man based on how he makes them feel <u>physically</u>. That's why women go crazy over male exotic dancers. A professional bodybuilder once told me that the reason women visit and marry men in prison is because of their muscular bodies. Too many men try to engage a man intellectually instead of physically. A man's physical attributes excite women, despite the nonsense put out in the media. If you see an otherwise intelligent woman with a dumb-ass man rest assured he has a buffed body.

Once off the dance floor, a man still needs to have good conversation skills. Since you followed my advice and broadened your mind and interests you should be able to have an intelligent conversation with any lady.

One thing I did when I used to go to clubs was that I usually left with one phone number. Why? **Quality over quantity.** By being selective I sent a subliminal message to the different women that I wasn't at the club to collect phone numbers. Women who checked me out realized that I wasn't trying to be a player. Quite frankly men chasing a bunch of phone numbers around look like jokes to women. Women want to feel special. They want to feel like all your attention was on them, even if deep down they know better. At the dance club focus your energy on the women you feel are most attractive. Don't collect a phone number if you are not feeling the woman. Forget trying to impress your buddies. Be very selective with women in the club and in general. (See Appendix II).

Going for the Best

In closing I want to say one thing: Go for the women you feel are the best. I emphasize the statement, **YOU FEEL ARE THE BEST**. If the best for you looks like Halle Berry or Angelina Jolie then go for it. If the best means going for a woman everybody else considers ugly but you feel she is the most beautiful woman in the world go for it. Don't short-change yourself. Most people will get into relationship or date people they consider mediocre and try to convince themselves that this is who they want. Don't lie to yourself. If you want a perfect ten go for it as long as you are willing to do what it takes to get a perfect 10. Other people will tell you to lower your standards but don't do it. You might be the man an Attractive Woman finds desirable.

Let me share a story with you. My freshman year in college I was sitting with some friends in the school cafeteria when this beautiful young lady walked by with her food. These guys found her stunning. Then I mentioned that I knew her and one guy proceeded to tell me how she wouldn't talk to somebody like me, that she was out of my league. I just let him talk. What he didn't know was that this girl helped me carry my bags to my dorm room during freshman orientation and that we had a class together and that we were good friends.

My point is that often a man gets get psyched out of approaching an Attractive Woman because he listens to his friends who are really scared themselves and feel like everyone should share their fears. Sometimes you may have to get new friends because many people refuse to grow.

One thing I need to say. An interesting thing will happen for the man who follows my advice in this and indeed the advice from all of my books. Instead of being able to get more women the man will get fewer women. The only saving grace about is that the women the man will get will be the extremely attractive ones. It's not that the average woman will not find you attractive. It's that they will find you so attractive that they will not trust your motives for approaching them. They will wonder, "What does this good-looking confident man want with me?" Even if you really like her she's not going to trust you without serious work on your part. Even if you manage to get into a relationship with her, she may play games or show other signs of insecurity.

Personally speaking, in my dealings with women, it was always the average woman who gave me hell, tried to play games, and even cheated on me. The attractive ones always treated me with kindness and respect. When I say attractive I don't mean just their physical appearance but their inner beauty. A beautiful spirit makes the plainest woman a ten.

The bottom line is this: be the best, go for the best, and make no apologies.

Peace,

Rom

APPENDIX I

A Woman's Choice

A key point in **Nice Guys and Players** is that women choose the men. A man must take his time to understand this concept. There are four ways in which women choose men.

A. Body Language

The most common way a woman chooses a man is through body language and other non-verbal techniques. The average woman is not going to walk up to a man and express a romantic interest in him. Women are more indirect than direct. Pages 22 through 26 of **Nice Guys and Players** outline the primary ways a woman will show her interest. The woman is hoping that the man will pick up on her interest and make the "first move." I used quotations because in reality the woman has made the first move in an indirect way.

Missing from the text are two very important indicators of a woman's interest. One is when a woman plays with her hair in your presence. There's a story behind why this is excluded.

Nice Guys and Players started out as an essay called **Nice Guy's Guide to Meeting and Attracting Beautiful Women.** I wanted a woman to read the guide to get her opinion. A woman I worked with agreed to read the essay. Before I gave it to her I deleted a reference I made about a woman playing with her hair in a man's presence. This particular woman consistently played with her hair in my presence. I didn't want her to know that I was reading her actions that well. I never got around to putting the information back into the text.

It's surprising how the average man doesn't know this simple indication.

The second important indicator left out of the text is when a woman makes an obvious effort not to look at the man. This is tricky as the case may be that the man repulses the woman. The trick is determining the context in which a woman is using this ploy. If a woman purposely looks away from a man she has been introduced to or has a passing acquaintance with, she probably is repulsed by him. In other cases if a woman is exhibiting this behavior with a man she doesn't know she is probably interested but trying to act like she is not. The key is this case is to "catch" her looking. If the woman is interested she is still going to want to look at you but she doesn't want to be caught looking at you. The way to do this is to learn how to use mirrors, reflective glass, and peripheral vision.

Depending on where you are, reflective surfaces can be used to catch a woman looking. For example, one day I was walking into a building when a couple of women walked past me. They didn't look at me nor smile. They gave no outward indication that they acknowledged my presence. I knew they liked what they saw because the doors of the building I was walking into had reflective surfaces and I could see them looking back. If I ran into them again I knew they would be receptive to an approach on my part. Also the use of peripheral vision is important if the woman is to the side of you. They may show a more obvious interest if they think you can't see them directly.

A woman using non-verbal and indirect signals is the most common way they will choose a man.

B. Aggressive Women

A growing percentage of women are directly aggressive in pursuit of the man of their choice. On one hand this is good because it takes the guesswork out of the equation. The man KNOWS this woman wants him. If she is appealing to the man he can seduce her easily. Actually, she is the one doing the seducing. On the other hand there are problems with this.

Two types of women are directly aggressive. One is a woman who is desperate and the other is a woman who tends to be controlling. The desperate woman will be easy to have sex with but in all likelihood other problems will surface which will indicate the reasons why she is desperate. Generally avoid this type of woman unless you REALLY need to get some and even then don't let her know where you live. A truly desirable woman will not be desperate as she has several men to choose from.

The other type of aggressive woman is one who will be controlling. A man will never be happy with a controlling woman because at some level she doesn't like men. Women choosing men in an aggressive manner is an obvious example of women choosing.

C. Availability

A woman may not give a man any signals and she may not be aggressive. Also a man may see a woman and do a cold approach. He may think he is the one doing the choosing but he's not. No matter what the man thinks, the woman is still choosing. For example, a man approaches two women in a day. These women have not provided any initial indication that they were interested in him. The first woman he approaches doesn't look at him and keeps walking at a brisk pace. She doesn't want to be bothered. The second woman stops and talks with the man in a friendly manner. The difference in the two scenarios is that the second woman made herself available for the man to talk to.

Availability is simply a woman making it easier for the man. This is especially true when a man already has a woman's phone number. With the advent of caller ID and cell phones women give out their numbers with more ease these days. In many cases a woman feel it is easier to give a man her phone number just to get him out of her face. They usually give the correct phone number because if a man sees her again he can't accuse her of giving him the wrong number. She can, however, refuse to take his phone calls and then play it off later.

A woman is exercising choice by returning phone calls, talking to the man on a consistent basis, and being available for dates. For example, a woman may talk to a man on the phone but will always be busy when he suggests getting together. For another man she will always be available for any of his suggestions. She is thus exercising a choice.

D. Society

Women as a group express their choice when there is a consensus on which men are considered attractive and which are not. Primarily peer groups and the media shape this consensus. An example in the case of peer groups is when a group of professional women in a book club decide that the ideal men are those who are professionals with good credit who are at least 6 feet tall with athletic bodies. As women are affected by the perception and opinions of their peers, a woman in this group will typically want a man who fits the group's criteria. A short, pudgy man with bad credit working as a part-time mechanic will not get the time of day from the women in this group.

The media also shapes a woman's choices. The ideal man for many women is the same type of man they see on television and in movies. Men who do not reach that ideal are not chosen. Subconsciously, women see the men and situations in the media as being real even though consciously they may know better. Their subconscious says this is what men are supposed to be like. The subconscious takes the information it receives as real. As a result many women have a romantic view of how men are supposed to behave. A man who doesn't behave this way is not chosen.

Learning to recognize the choice.

A man must learn how to recognize the choice. A practical exercise in this regard is going to a nightclub or any other place where there are men and women and simply observe the dynamics. A reasonably intelligent man should be able to pick up on women choosing different men. Another exercise for a man is to simply be quiet and pay attention to how women generally behave around him in everyday situations. He will get an idea about who finds him attractive.

An important aspect of a man learning how to recognize the choice is to get out of the habit of going for the first woman he thinks is fine. The man in this regard should learn to enter a particular situation and observe everything going on. An exercise in this regard is to go into a club and purposely wait a half-hour to an hour before saying anything to a woman. In this way the man develops the patience necessary to pay attention to what's going on and he also learns to calm down and think rationally as opposed to being led by his libido.

The Man's Choice

Most men, when told that women make the initial choice, think they are powerless to get the woman of their choice. What a man doesn't realize is that he has more power. When a man chooses a woman SHE has the power. He has to meet HER conditions for dating. He mistakenly thinks that he is convincing her with dinners, flowers, and shopping sprees. She has total control because SHE has what he wants and she has decided a price, which in all likelihood she hasn't shared with him. Only when he pays HER price does he get anything. Men are deluded when they think they are choosing the woman. Think about the following statement:

> If men were doing the choosing, would a man voluntarily spend money, lie, cheat, and steal to have sex with a woman? He would get with her on HIS terms and not hers. Valentine's Day would not exist. Indeed, a major part of the economy would not exist.

When a man acknowledges that women choose the men and acts on this knowledge he gains power in several ways. One, he stops wasting time with women who do not want him. He can focus his energy on women who do want him. A man will gain power because once a woman chooses a man she will tend to always want that man and in many cases will do what it takes to get him. The key here is realizing that though a woman chooses, the man must **accept** the choice. For example a woman sends signals to a man and he ignores her. Women by nature do not give up easily once they want a man. She will try harder to get his attention. He becomes a challenge to her and many women prefer a man who presents a challenge. A smart man will see this and will be able to get anything out of her. There is a role reversal in a sense. The woman will be doing everything in her power to convince him to choose her. In this way a man is dealing with a woman on HIS terms.

Now a man may feel like he may not want the woman who will choose him. He wants who he wants, choice or not. There are two ways of looking at this. One is that he will have trouble with a woman who hasn't chosen him. She is not going to date him anyway and if she does she will try to use him. Two, in many cases the woman who chooses the man is somebody the man will want. This brings us to a key point of **Nice Guys and Players**:

A man is working to become the type of man that the average woman will be inclined to choose.

A reality is that women want supermen. They want alpha males. This is going to be the case regardless of all the intellectual nonsense in the media. In fact, if you pay close attention to the media this is what you see. The media images are based on a woman's primal desires. If women desired short, fat dumpy men that's what we would see in the media.

APPENDIX II

Secrets of the Select

In *Nice Guys and Players* and *Sexual Chemistry* I talked about the four main categories of men in terms of how women classify them. The categories are listed as follows:

Mr. Goodbar

Select. Handsome with good looks and body build. Raw sex appeal.

Masked Men

Select. Don't have the raw sex appeal of Mr. Goodbar. May be handsome with good body build. Main attraction is above average income and status.

Nice Guys
Non-Select.   Bland and clueless.   Lacks raw sex appeal. Women keep them as platonic friends.

Gamesmen
Non-Select. Lacks looks, money or sex appeal. Can get women only through tricks and persistence.

The men who women want attention from are Mr. Goodbars and Masked Men. Now on the surface it seems like women want these men because they are handsome with lots of money. Being handsome with lots of money does influence many women. No man can go wrong by improving his physical appearance and having a well-paying job. Hold-up though. For every rule there are exceptions. There are rare Mr. Goodbars who physically ugly, no muscles and broke. On the other hand there are rare Nice Guys who are handsome, muscular, and are millionaires. The reality is that there is only one trait that truly separates the Select from the non-select: The Select men are **SELECTIVE** as to the women they will deal with.

Selectivity is the key to having the right to be a member of the Select. Mr. Goodbar and the Masked Man don't necessarily get the most women. Gamesmen get the most women because they play a numbers game. A Gamesmen will hit on 100 women in month. Out of that number he may sleep with five of them. Five women a month may seem great until one realizes that the Gamesman is dealing women who tend to be ugly, overweight, skinny, crazy, and have low self-esteem. Quite frankly sex is easy to get for a man who has no real standards in a woman other than that she has a pulse.

The Select get the best quality women. The Select don't chase after women. Women chase after them. The Select tap into a woman's desire to be with the best man. In addition since the percentage of Select Men is relatively small, there is much competition for their attention. Thus this dynamic stimulates a woman's competitive nature. Women need to feel like they won the challenge of getting a Select Man to give them attention. Women like the feeling of getting a man who rejects other women.

The problem with many men is that they feel they must hit on every woman they encounter. They don't realize that women exclude them from serious consideration at this point. Women aren't stupid. They know if a man is playing a game. Women see through these games and turn things around. That's when a man looks up and wonders if he is such a player why these women are not rushing to be with him. These men wonder why a woman will stop going out with them on slight provocations. For example, a woman will stop dealing with a Gamesman if he is so much as five minutes late for a date. The same woman will only go out with a Nice Guy if he willing to spend hundreds of dollars on her at the most expensive restaurant. Now when the same woman encounters Mr. Goodbar, she will let him get away with being three hours late, pay his way on a date, and cook dinner for him.

The Select Men have standards. If a woman doesn't meet those standards, the Select will not deal with her. The Select are not pressed. They deal with women on their terms and not the woman's. When they go to clubs, they will leave with one phone number. That phone number will be from the most attractive woman in the place. The Select believe in quality over quantity.

This is why *Nice Guys and Players* and *Sexual Chemistry* focused more on self-development than on women. The Select are more concerned with living life on their terms than adjusting their personality to run game on women.

To find out more about Rom Wills, to read his blog, and purchase his other books go to:

www.romwills.com

www.ingramcontent.com/pod-product-compliance
Lightning Source LLC
Chambersburg PA
CBHW071413040426
42444CB00009B/2231